T0328495

The Visa

Mohamed Combo Kamanda

The Visa

ISBN: 3-9808084-7-5

First published 2007
Sierra Leonean Writers Series
c/o Mallam O. & J. Enterprises
120 Kissy Road, Freetown, Sierra Leone
publisher@sl-writers-series.org
www.sl-writers-series.org

Characters

Eku	(President of African students' association - ASA)
Marion	(Eku's spouse)
Martha, Marian Marie and Amy	(Children of Eku and Marion)
Abou	(Social Secretary of ASA)
Angela	(An African student, now a British citizen)
Uche	(A newly arrived student from Africa)
Priscilla	(Treasurer of ASA)
Kisa	(Priscilla's husband)
Ibrahim	(A member of ASA who has completed his studies)
Maama	(Ibrahim's spouse)
Ansu	(Ibrahim and Maama's son)
Pa Ayoka	(Maama's father)
Sisi Ada	(Maama's mother)
Pa Oni	(Maama's uncle)
Alhaji Moidawu	(A learned Qur'anic teacher)
Pastor Jaaka	(A church minister)
Young Man	To be played by a member of the cast
Masquerades	
1st Client	To be played by any member of the cast
2nd Client	To be played by any member of the cast
1st Secretary	To be played by any member of the cast
2nd secretary	To be played by any member of the cast

White male

Waiters and Waitresses	To be played by members of the cast
Sharon	To be played by any member of the cast
Abraham	(A figment of Eku's imagination)
Carol	(Another figment of Eku's imagination)
Daniel	(Carol's friend, also a figment of Eku's imagination)
Registrar	(Another figment of Eku's imagination)

SYNOPSIS

This play highlights some of the consequences of UK visa restrictions on international students from sub-Saharan Africa; it also examines the ways in which these students respond to the challenges posed by immigration rules and the new culture.

Eku, Abou, Priscilla and Ibrahim are university lecturers in their countries of origin who are currently pursuing postgraduate degrees in the UK. For Eku, the brutal and savage rebel war in his country (Sierra Leone) necessitates that he must bring his children to safety in the UK. However, he has neither the financial resources to obtain air tickets, nor the visas for his children without assistance. On the other hand, although Ibrahim has the means to acquire a UK visa and air ticket for Maama, his wife, the latter is too critically pregnant to be able to travel together with her husband. As a result, Maama's trip to the UK is postponed. One month after safely delivering their son, Maama and the child set off for the UK -to be reunited with her husband, Ibrahim. While on transit in a North African country, their journey is aborted because the child has no visa to be allowed entry into the UK! Although Priscilla encounters no difficulties in her visa application for her husband, Kisa, the change of the husband's role in the new culture from breadwinner to housekeeper proves to be a humbling experience, particularly for Uche who is fresh from Africa.

The play is in two acts. Act one, *Orientating new arrivals*, focuses on how members of the African Students Association (ASA) assist other African students to settle down in a new culture. Act two, *A student's Private life*, highlights the difficulties that students and their families face in acquiring visas for overseas travel. It also briefly focuses on how an African male accepts change of roles in marriage. The concluding scene, *Denouement*, centres on the implications of *'student visa'* in the textbox below. The scene also highlights ways in which successful international students who would like to overstay their leave to remain, circumvent immigration rules in order to be eligible for employment.

A UK STUDENT VISA READS AS FOLLOWS:

Leave to remain in the United Kingdom, on condition that the holder maintains and accommodates himself and any dependants without recourse to public funds, does not enter or change employment paid or unpaid without the consent of the Secretary of State for the Home Department is hereby given until --

on behalf of the Secretary of State

Home Office

Act One

Scene One

Planning a Welcome Party

The setting is Eku's departmental office in the UK, furnished with office chairs and tables, a filing cabinet, computer and printer, and a telephone set. There are also a notice board, bookshelves and a filing cabinet. Eku is middle-aged and a modest gentleman of medium height. He speaks English, Krio and Nigerian Pidgin. A very time-conscious person, Eku is also a highly emotional character. Eku's national sentiments are exemplified by his love for indigenous costumes and display of national symbols, such as his country's flag, copies of the national anthem and national pledge that he conspicuously displays on the office wall. Eku is usually a cautious person and can be indecisive at crucial moments. He speaks with authority and in a measured way. His severe look sometimes disguises his good humour. Presently, Eku enters and places his bag on his table, slumps into a chair in front of the computer table and starts the computer. After a brief while, the telephone rings.

Eku: *(Picks up the phone)* Hello... Ah! <u>Maahsa</u>! I received your message from the receptionist... I was surprised because I wasn't expecting you to be in school today. *(He listens with a grin).* Honestly, I thought you would be down with hangover from the weekend's enjoyment. *(He listens).* It's a shame we couldn't attend this year's African-Caribbean Night... I beg your pardon. *(He listens pensively).* Oh no! It's nothing to do with my sentiments against...*(Presently, there is a knock on the door).* Hang on a sec... *(He puts the handset aside and hurries to open the door).*

(Angela, Uch,e Abou and Priscilla enter. Angela speaks with an accent and the fluency of a native English lady. She is very argumentative and casual about appearances. Uche is tall, soft-spoken and very calculated. His freshness in the UK is typified by his safari suit, pidgin expressions and a strong Nigerian accent of English. Abou is well built, buoyant and an

assertive person. Priscilla is cool, soft-spoken, stern and obsessed with her appearance. Eku indicates the seats to his guests. They sit and try to occupy themselves, by either reading newspapers or miming the action of conversing).

Eku: Please make yourselves comfortable. It's Ibrahim on the line *(He picks up the phone)*

Angela: *(Curiously)* What's Ibrahim up to? Surely, he hasn't forgotten we should be meeting here in your office today at 12.00 mid-day.

Eku: *(Ignores Angela's interruption and continues to listen)* As I was saying, we couldn't attend because we were away on a family visit to Edinburgh. By the way, Abou and other members of the executive are already here for the scheduled meeting. *(He listens).* Okay. See you soon, …bye. *(He replaces the handset).*

Abou: *(In a lively and cordial tone)* <u>Chief, doctor, Alhaji…nah waa oo</u>.

Eku: *(Excitedly)* My dear brother, how are you?

Abou: Chief! <u>Ah jus de</u>. *(He introduces Eku to Uche)* Uche, meet the man we call 'counsellor'. *(Uche gets up, shakes hands with and greets Eku)* Eku is our chairman and also a PhD candidate in language education. Uche is newly arrived from Nigeria to pursue M.Phil. /PhD in soil science.

Angela: *(To Uche, in jest)* Uche, please don't end up as a nurse or taxi driver in this country after learning everything about soil science… *(They laugh about it).*

Eku: *(chuckles and changes the topic)* Anyway, Uche, you are very welcome to England. When did you arrive?

Uche: About two weeks ago.

Eku: *(To Abou)* Uhuh, so, how did you meet Uche?

Abou: We met at the local British Council office and have been in touch ever since. We went together to the African Caribbean night last weekend.

Eku: I see, you must have had good fun...

Angela and Priscilla: *(Sarcastically)* Fun is the word...

Abou: What? *(Directing the question at Angela and Priscilla)*

Angela and Priscilla: *(Ignore the inquisition.)*

Uche: Oh yes! I met quite a good number of Africans, listened to some Afro beats, Dombolo and other kinds of African music; I also ate sumptuous exotic African dishes.

Eku: Uhuh! You must be settling down well ...

Uche: Well, it's too early to judge. As you know it's not easy. Thanks to the weather and other family problems back home.
Abou: One rule about the British weather is that one must always be prepared for it. It is very unpredictable.

Angela: Oh yes! You can have all four seasons in one day. Hence, always carry your warm clothing with you.

Eku: Quite often, people from hot climates like Africa's, contract pneumonia and other forms of respiratory diseases, due to the cold.

Priscilla: I always remember the final words of advice from the International Students' Advice and Welfare Officer on *International Students Day* in 1991, 'Don't worry about how you may look to other people. Always make sure that you're properly protected against the cold weather', she warned. That has always been my guiding principle.

Angela: Also, drink as much fluid as you can, hot and cold.

Eku: That reminds me; brothers and sisters what can I get you, tea or coffee?

Abou: Black tea for me, please.

Angela: White coffee and two sugars for me, please.

Abou: Black coffee and no sugar for me, please.

Uche: *(Amused).* 'White or black coffee?' *(Indignantly)* Can you drink tea or coffee without sugar?

Eku: *(Chuckles)* You scientists know more about why sugar intake needs to be controlled.

Uche: *(Indifferently)* Of course, but I will still have white tea and three sugar cubes.

(All with the exception of Uche laugh about the colour of tea, coffee and type of sugar, while Eku exits).

Angela: You, Abou!

Abou: *(Surprised)* What!

Angela: I haven't forgotten about the comments you made at the bus stop yesterday. I still believe that this trip to Europe will help Africans like you, understand that women are more than mere pieces of property.

Priscilla: They're all the same, educated or not. Take my partner, Kisa, for an example, who still thinks we are in Africa where I used to take his socks off from his feet, or kneel down to serve his meals.

Angela: *(Contemptuously)* Over my dead body!

Abou: *(Sarcastically)* Priscilla, please don't behave like the child who can remember where it fell down, but not where it slipped before the fall.

Angela: *(impressed)* What does that mean, guru of proverbs?

Priscilla: *(Impatiently)* But trust me! I am helping him to learn how to treat his wife as a partner, rather than as a piece of property.

Angela: *(Scornfully)* Medieval savage! Is Kisa not learning anything from other African male colleagues, or the TV programmes?

Uche: *(butts in)* It amazes me how easily some people change into a fish because they are thrown into a river…

(Angela and Priscilla look in Uche's direction in amazement. Almost simultaneously, Eku re-enters with the drinks and distributes them accordingly, interjecting in the discussion as he does so)

Eku: I don't need any lessons on marriage at my age.

Abou: *(Sternly)* Particularly not from apostles of feminism …

Uche: 'Woman libe', as we call them in Nigeria

Angela: I beg your pardon!

Priscilla: Do you mean there's nothing of benefit you could learn from women's fight for equal rights or other polemical discussions in the media?

Eku: *(Derisively)* Of course, there is!

Angela: You guys need to grow up! Why do you talk as if Africa is a model for moral uprightness?

Abou: Look here, Angela! Even in my wildest dream, I wouldn't imagine that. My point is that not all that glitters in this country is gold.

(At present, Ibrahim's knock on the door distracts everyone; he is welcome by Eku. Ibrahim is generally a shrewd and foppish young man; he never minces his words. Presently, he is uncharacteristically quiet and withdrawn.)

Eku: Oh, that was quick!

Abou: *(He clears his throat)* What have you been up to?

Priscilla: You look unwell, what's the matter?

Ibrabim: *(Indifferently)* Priscilla, I'm okay …

Eku: They are pulling your legs. Can I get you something?

Ibrahim: No, thanks.

Eku: *(To Angela and Priscilla)* Anyway, you gender activists may have to look for another platform; now that Ibrahim is here we must get down to business. *(To Ibrahim)* As you may be aware, this meeting cannot wait because Angela is due to attend a conference in Johannesburg. When is it?

Angela: In two weeks' time.

Eku: Good luck, Angie.

All: Good luck, dear.

Eku: Shall we call this meeting to order? *(Pauses)* Let's refer to the minutes of the last meeting. I hope we have all received and read our copies, apart from Uche *(He passes Uche a copy of the minutes and allows him some time to skim through)*. Matters arising from the minutes…

Angela: Page 2, paragraph 2, line 3. Check the spelling of 'privilege'.

Eku: *(To Ibrahim)* Take note, IB.

Ibrahim: *(He nods in approval)* Thanks, Angie.

Eku: Any other matters? *(After a reasonable pause)* Okay, straight to the main item on the agenda, 'The Welcome Party'. Abou, you may update the house on the progress to date.

Abou: *(He clears his throat again)* I have tentatively booked the Palmers' musical set, complete with DJs and performers. Amazingly, they have a good collection of African music. I have made arrangements with the SU press for different forms of advert. FM 113.2 has offered us some airtime, 10 times a day from the 15th of October. The local Newspaper, *The Southern Echo*, has also offered to advertise the party in the last two weeks of October. I have applied for fliers and other kinds of poster. That's it. *(Indicates that he's finished)*.

Eku: Thanks chief.

Angela: May I continue from there?

Eku: You may.

Angela: According to the Student Union records, there are 30 indigenous African students. Fortunately, we have been able to contact all of them. One of them *(Referring to Uche)* is here with us.

Eku: Brilliant.

Priscilla: What date are we aiming at?

Abou: Wouldn't the first Saturday in November be ideal? The fresh men and women would have settled down, and ...

Eku: There will be some money in our accounts to spend *(They all consent).*

Ibrahim: So, shall we pencil down the 6th of November?

All: *(Consent verbally or by nodding approval).*

Angela: Venue is the SU Ballroom.

Ibrahim: *(To Abou)* Have you already paid for the musical system?

Abou: Not yet. The treasurer and I will do so after this meeting, or tomorrow at the very latest.

Eku: Good! Angela and Priscilla will take care of refreshments. Would that be okay with you? *(Looking in their direction)*

Angela and Priscilla: *(Sarcastically)* Yeh, yeh, ladies in the kitchen, that'll be fine.

Eku: Please don't start...

Ibrahim: Also, we should make our own arrangements for security. Last year was a bit dodgy, with many gatecrashers and lager louts that became intolerable in the end.

Priscilla: *(Humorously)* Abou can make a very good bouncer considering his build...

Eku: *(With a giggle)* Well, chief, shall we rely on you for sorting out the security situation?

Abou: That'll be fine.

Eku: Fabulous! A.O.B.

Abou: *(Clears his throat)* Racial harassment has resumed in earnest ...

Angela: You sound as if problems of racial abuse actually disappear ...

Abou: *(ignores Angela)* One of our members complained of racial discrimination at the student bar in one of the halls of residence. Another also complains of being constantly harassed by a group of young children on her way to the hostel. They make noises at her and sometimes throw stones in her path.

Priscilla: That's serious...

Eku: Racial matters are very sensitive. The *Student Advice and Welfare Officers* or the police will usually ask for details such as the date, time and identity of person or persons involved in the incident, and so on.

Angela: Besides, as 'coloured people', it's better to avoid putting ourselves in harm's way...

Eku: Absolutely!

Angela: You guys talk as if victims of racial attacks are the ones to blame; you don't need to court the attention of racist thugs…

Abou: We know this, Angie.

Eku: I recall that when I joined the ASA two years ago, one of our sisters went on a night out alone. She went to a pub located in an area specified by the British Council as dangerous for international study fellows. It seems that this lady did not only ignore that warning, she also had more pints of beer in that dangerous pub than she required for the night…

Angela: I think I've heard of this incident once.

Abou: *(Tapping Angela on her shoulder)* Please allow those who haven't heard it before to benefit from the experience.

Eku: Anyway, when our sister recovered from the assault, she wanted the ASA to help her fight a racial case against the owners of the pub. For goodness sake, if you know that someone is looking to roast you, you don't cover yourself in oil and sit by a fire!

Priscilla: You guys, doesn't your stock of proverbs ever run dry?

Uche: In Nigeria, we say, 'If you're suffering from epilepsy, don't play by the fireside.'

Eku: Anyway, my advice to everybody is that we shouldn't put ourselves in harm's way. Being international students, we are ambassadors of our respective countries. Whether we are the victims or perpetrators of a crime, the resulting stigma is often attributed more to our nationalities than to our individual identities. That Sierra Leonean, Ghanaian, Nigerian or Zambian student has been involved in such and such, they would say. Anything else? *(Pauses and looks around)* Well, in the absence of any other business, can someone move that this meeting be adjourned?

Angela: I so do.

Eku: This meeting is adjourned. Thank you all for coming. Hope to see you on or before the 6th of November. *(To Ibrahim)* IB, can I have a word?

(All disperse, leaving Eku and Ibrahim on the stage centre. As they murmur, the lights fade out on them).

End of Scene

****

Scene Two

At the Student Union Refectory

(The setting is the Student Union Refectory. Different foods, drinks and adverts of various items could be seen on display. Contemporary music and the noise of students fill the background. Students queue up in single files to the counter. Now and again, a waiter or waitress comes up and asks customers for orders. Eku, Angela, Priscilla, Abou and Uche are next in the queue. Presently, Eku, Angela and Priscilla have ordered their choice of food and drinks and found suitable sitting accommodation for five. It's Uche's turn to put in an order. In a flash, a white male student arrogantly jumps the queue and starts to put in his order. Abou recognises the misnomer and vehemently intervenes).

Abou: Excuse me...

White Male: Whoh?

Abou: Do you realise we're in a queue?

(At first, the white male ignores Abou's mild protest, and continues to place the order. Presently, Angela notices the affront and joins Abou and Uche at the counter).

Angela: *(Visibly angry and unable to disguise it. She addresses the waiter)* This is discrimination in a higher institution of learning, of all places! It's Uche's turn to be served, and you should serve him before anyone else!

Waiter: *(Shocked and embarrassed)* I'm terribly sorry. I thought it was this gentleman's turn to be served *(Referring to the white male).*

(Meanwhile, the white male moves behind Uche, muttering indistinct obscenities as he does so).

Angela: I will accept that excuse if you're blind *(She retorts, returning triumphantly to her seat).*

Waiter: *(To Uche)* Oh! Hello. Good afternoon. How can I help you, sir?

Uche: Errm. I want that *(Indicating).*

Waiter: What do you want, sir?

Uche: That! *(Indicating the food item that Eku and others had ordered).*

Waiter: Which one? *(Trying to ridicule Uche).*

Abou: *(Says the name of the food item in Uche's ear)* It's a baguette.

Waiter: *(Almost with a giggle)* Oh! I see. You want a chicken and curry baguette, chicken and curry baguette! *(Repeating for emphasis. The waiter picks the baguette and places it in a disposable plate).* Anything else sir?

Uche: Yes, a can of coke, please

Waiter: Thank you very much. You may pay over there! *(Indicating the cashier).*

-*(Uche moves over to the cashier, pays for the food and drink and joins the others).*

Waiter: Who's next please?

Abou: I want 2 scones, chicken and chips and a bottle of water, please.

Waiter: Certainly! *(He picks the food items requested and puts them in a disposable plate. As she gives Abou the plate)* You should know where to pay, shouldn't you?

Abou: *(Ignores the patronising comment)*

(Abou pays for the food and drink and joins the others. As he does so, the characters and action at the counter freeze. It's Uche's turn to break the silence).

Uche: As well as that young man's rude behaviour towards me, I didn't know the names of some of the food on display.

Eku: You shouldn't let that bother you at all. You think those waiters and waitresses know about *gari, foofoo, or agbono soup*? You will know about these food varieties as time goes on. I have lived in this country for more than three years now, yet, there are still many things about British culture that I know very little about.

Abou: We have all had our fair share of embarrassments in this country

Eku: My first culture shock was at the Bed & Breakfast where I stayed for the first week. It was during breakfast; I had ordered cooked breakfast, thinking it was the good old plate of rice and any familiar sauce. So, even after eating the full English breakfast: 2 sausages, 2 slices of bacon, one fried egg, tomato and mushroom, I sat waiting for my imaginary cooked breakfast. The landlady, realising that I still sat expectantly, demanded if there was anything more she could do for me. 'I am waiting for the cooked breakfast, madam'. I told her. *(Humorously)* 'You've just had it', she said. *(Everyone laughed with the exception of Uche)*

Angela: *(Laughing uncontrollably)* Eku, you will kill me with these stories.

Ibrahim: I must have told some of you about my own experience with the duvet.

Priscilla: Not me.

Angela: *(Amused)* Ah! You and that story about the duvet.

Ibrahim: *(Ignores the question)* As you are aware, in Africa we use light cover-cloth to protect us from the cold and mosquitoes.

Abou: Of what use would a duvet be in a tropical climate?

Ibrahim: Fine! Then you'll understand why I slept on it, thinking it was part of the comfort a bed in the UK can offer to an African. The following morning I wasted no time in registering my protest to the landlady.

(All except Uche, burst out laughing wildly at the implied ignorance)

Angela: You may have noticed queues wherever you go: here at the refectory, the bank, bus stops, library, you name it. For someone from the chaos in my own country, queues were my own greatest culture shock. I experienced my greatest embarrassment at the Student Travel Centre. I thought I could muscle my way to the front of the queue as we would normally do back home, and get away with it. Unfortunately, the Ticket Assistant was smarter, 'Do you realise there is a queue here?' Almost dumb-founded, I apologised and retreated to the rear.

Uche: Goodness me!

Ibrahim: Culture shock in this country takes different forms, my dear brother. I remember the Cameroonian gentleman who thought that the landlady of a pub that constantly referred to him as 'My Love', 'My Dear' and 'Darling', was genuinely announcing her affection for him. Little did he realise that the lady was merely mouthing meaningless phrases.

Uche: *(Apparently overwhelmed)* Well! <u>Nah waaa ooo</u>!

(After a brief while)

Eku: *(To Uche)* Did you like the baguette?

Uche: *(Visibly thrilled by Ibrahim's account. After a brief pause)* Well, it's not the same as yams or foofoo<u>, boht how man go do</u>?

Eku: One of these days, you must join my family for an African dinner. I will discuss it with Marion, my wife, and will get back to you.

Uche: <u>Oga, tank you plenty, plenty</u>.

(Waiters frantically clearing the tables of leftovers, empty plates, cups and cutlery distract him)

Uche: *(Curiously)* What are they going to do with all those leftovers?

Angela: Bin them. Why?

Uche: My God! There is so much wastage here...

Eku: Wastage!

Angela: Who will eat leftovers?

Eku: Pigs do.

Ibrahim: *(Calmly)* Oh yes. *(Almost at the same time that Uche exclaims)*

Ibrahim: Oh yes! Leftovers like those are used for making pigswill.

Uche: *(Puzzled)* Aha. May be, that's why the pigs here are so fat…

(The music rises to a crescendo as waiters and waitresses move in frenzy. Eku, Abou, Angela and the rest finish their food and drinks. Everyone gets up, tucks his/her chair in, exchanges handshake and observes other courtesies of parting. Uche remains glued to his seat, looking pensively as waiters and waitresses clear the dining tables.

Uche: *(Alone on stage centre with lights focused on him)* P..i..g…s.. will! *(Laughs cynically)* Hmmmm.

(Lights fade)

End of Scene

****

Scene Three

The Welcome Party

The hall is decorated with ribbons, balloons and a world map on which Africa is highlighted. Also on display are flags of the different nationalities and banners on which are boldly inscribed the following: 'ASA Welcomes You All'; 'Welcome to the South Coast' 'ASA, Here to Serve Your Needs'; ASA, the Organisation to Turn to'; ASA, the Shoulder to Lean on'; 'Are You African? You Are Not Alone'. Stage lights, the blare of contemporary music and the buzz of party revellers set the scene. At one end of the hall is the high table, indicated by decorations, flower vases, bottles of drinks and wine glasses, etc. Each other table with 3 to 4 chairs around it, is delicately prepared, on which is placed some bottles of wine, cans or pints of beer and soft drink. As the invited guests arrive, they take their seats assigned to them by members of the executive. Presently, Abou, the social secretary of ASA walks over to the DJ and mutters instructions; the music dies down, punctuated by brightening of lights in the hall. As the party organisers take their seats on the high table, Abou uses the microphone to address the audience).

Abou: *(In a bubbly demeanour and tone of voice)* Our brothers and sisters who have newly arrived from home, distinguished ladies and gentlemen, on behalf of ASA, I welcome you all. I can sense the eagerness on your faces to share in the exotic meals and rhythms of Africa, but first things first. Tonight's programme of events is on each table. The first item is prayers for which I now call upon Uche to lead us.

Uche: Shall we all stand! In silence, let's pray for our different needs and intentions in our own ways. *(Pauses for a couple of minutes)* Amen/amen

Abo: I will call on Angela, one of architect's of this occasion, to introduce the president of ASA who also doubles as chair of this night's proceedings. Angela.

Angela: Goodevening to you all. The chair of tonight's proceedings is very well known to most of you in this hall. You can easily identify him by his charm, warmth and eagerness to help, wherever and whenever. If you were a freshman or lady who worships at the university's Chapel, you would have noticed a well-built, dignified looking, middle-aged Eucharistic minister. You may have also met our chairman at the Student Union Building in the International Students' Welfare Office or at the Union bar with his pint of Fosters, involved in verbal political feuds; you really can't miss him. He is a Sierra Leonean Commonwealth Scholar, pursuing PhD in language Education, formerly a university lecturer in his country of origin. Ladies and gentlemen, our chairman is Mr. Eku Scotland.

Eku: Thanks for those 'compliments', Angela. The International Students' Welfare Officer, executives of ASA, distinguished ladies and gentlemen, freshmen and ladies from Africa; I am particularly honoured to welcome you all to our first social event of this academic year. The African Students' Association that was established 5 years ago, compliments the services of the International Students' Welfare team of the Students' Union, ably represented tonight by Sharon *(indicating her)*. Look around the walls of this hall and read what the banners say *(pauses):* those statements encapsulate the key roles of this association. You may have noticed that England does not have streets paved with gold, or trees that bear British pounds as fruits for easy picking. On the contrary, England is a country like any other; you work, toil and labour to earn your living. You shouldn't be under any illusions about the challenges that lie ahead of you. You mustn't be fooled by the neon lights, the plastic smiles or efficiency of the buses and trains. We know you are all mature, experienced and conscientious folks to be fooled by these. However, from experience, we also do know that you may need help to get your head round some culture specific issues that are bound to confront you. Our key message to you this evening is that if you are in any difficulty, if you need advice on matters such as holiday jobs, visa application for your dependants, leisure and entertainment, feel free to contact any member of our executive or any existing member of ASA; although office hours on Monday to Friday in the Student union building are preferable, you are very welcome to contact us via phone or email at any time. Surely, it is unfair to take away from the precious time we have for eating, drinking and dancing. If you have any queries, please do not hesitate to ask me, or any member of the executive, distinguished by their badges. Once more, you are all very welcome to the UK; I wish you a very successful and trouble free stay during the course of your programme. On behalf of the executive, I formally declare this party open. DINNER IS SERVED!! IT'S SELF SERVICE, SO, EAT OR YOU STARVE!

(Presently, the sound of classical African music can be heard in the background. Angela, Priscilla and other members of the executive uncover the food and invite the guests, beginning with ladies. In queues the guests self-serve themselves and return to their seats. Participants eat, or mime the action of eating, chatting or interacting lively as the music continues to play in the background. After a while, the music changes from classical African to a faster 'Rumba', 'Makossa' or 'Dombolo' genre. Disco lights intermittently flash to establish a change of atmosphere. Eku and Angela open the dance floor, then the party moves into the next gear, then into full swing. After a while, Abou goes over to the DJ and mumbles instructions. A series of slow, romantic choice of music signal the end of the party; invited guests shake hands or mime the action of departing courtesies while the party organisers start packing up. Lights fade to signal the end of the scene).

Scene four

(One month later)

At The Job Centre

(Abou is assisting Uche to acquire part-time employment. They are formally dressed for this occasion. At the Job Centre, they meet other job seekers. There are notice boards with classified job adverts, both skilled and unskilled vacancies. Prospective applicants are required to look at the adverts and select vacancies that suit their qualifications or job experiences. There are three· terminals, manned by three secretaries responsible for assisting job seekers. Each of the secretaries in the lounge is seated behind a separate table. On each table are accessories such as a computer monitor, keyboard, printer, telephone set, filing trays for 'IN' and 'OUT' documents, and a huge address-book. Priscilla, Abou and Uche are among the early arrivals. They are ahead of the queue. At present, only one of the secretaries (all of them white English girls) is free, the others are busy on the telephone. Each of the secretaries speaks the accent of English spoken in Southern England).

1st Secretary: Who is next please?

Priscilla: *(Moves over and sits in the chair in front of the Secretary's table).* Good morning.

1st Secretary: *(Melodiously)* Hello! How can I help you?

Priscilla: *(Presenting a list of job vacancies to the secretary)* I am a university student looking for temporary employment in any of the vacancies listed *(Indicating the vacancies written on a piece of paper).*

1st Secretary: Lovely! Do you have any form of identification on you, please?

Priscilla: *(Produces her National Insurance Number and hands it over to the secretary).*

1st Secretary: *(Inspects the NI Card)* Your NI card is not proof of identity. I need your passport, a driving licence or student identity card.

Priscilla: *(Produces her passport)* Here you are, then.

1st Secretary: Lovely! *(She flips through the pages of the passport).* Okay then. *(Routinely talks to herself and Priscilla as she completes a form in front of her)* And you have the National Insurance Number. Good! Now, then... Have you identified any vacancies that suit your qualifications?

Priscilla: Yes. *(Hand over to the secretary).*

1st Secretary: Excellent! *(She chuckles as she examines the options)* This is how it works. I will call each of these Departments and will let you know what they say. Is that okay? Fingers crossed.

1st Secretary: *(Takes the telephone handset and dials)* Oh! Hello. This is Louise from the Job Centre. I have Mrs. *(She looks at the identification documents on the table and struggles to pronounce the name)* Muwuta.

Priscilla: Mututwa, please!

1st Secretary: Oh! Sorry about that. *(She makes a desperate effort)* I have Mrs. Mututa here; she is interested in the post of Administrative Assistant you advertised with us. *(She listens, and makes another desperate effort).* Mumuwuta

Priscilla: Mututwa, please!

1st Secretary: Mrs Mututuwa. *(To Priscilla)* I'm sorry. *(She listens)* Aha. Okay. Okay. Aha. No, not at all! That's fine. I'll tell her.

Okaydoki. Cheers. Bye. *(She turns to Priscilla)* I'm afraid the first choice of vacancy has already gone.

Priscilla: But why is the post still advertised at the Job Centre?

1st Secretary: *(Unable to disguise her embarrassment)* Erm, these things happen, you know. It's possible that the vacancy was filled as soon as it was advertised. Anyway, I'll try the second vacancy if that's okay with you.

Priscilla: Go ahead.

1st Secretary: *(She dials and listens)* Oh, hello! This is Louise from the Job Centre. I have Mrs. *(She looks at the identification documents again)* Mututa…

Priscilla: Mututwa, please!

1st Secretary: *(Less politely)* Sorry about that.

Priscilla: That's okay.

1st Secretary: I've a female student here with me, applying for the part-time post of Social Worker in your establishment. *(She listens)* Aha. Aha. Okay. No, no, not at all. That's fine; will do. Okaydo. Thanks. Bye. *(She replaces the hand set and turns to Priscilla)* Erm… I'm afraid; the second vacancy is also no longer available. I wonder what's happening today.

(The secretary vainly looks at Priscilla, the latter becoming increasingly impatient).

1st Secretary: *(Tentatively)* shall we try the third vacancy?

Priscilla: *(She heaves a sigh).* Okay.

1st Secretary: You can see that I'm doing my best. It's just that so far, nothing seems to be working in our favour. Anyway, let's keep our fingers crossed. *(She crosses her two middle fingers as she dials the third number. She listens)* Oh, hello! This is Louise from the Job Centre. I've Mrs... *(She looks blankly at Priscilla).*

Priscilla: Mututwa, please!

1st Secretary: *(Still looking at Priscilla)* I've a female student here with me applying for the part-time post of Kitchen Porter in your Hotel. *(She listens, and then responds with excitement)* Aha! Jolly Good! *(Looks at Priscilla and smiles animatedly).* Fantastic! Okay do. I'll tell her. Will do. Okay do. Thank you very much. Bye. *(Excited, she turns to Priscilla)* Well! At last, it seems we are getting somewhere. The Chef is very happy to inform you that the vacancy still exists. He's pleased to interview you for the post at the earliest possibility; meaning, if you're available even this minute, you could be interviewed. Ermm... you may however need the names and addresses of two referees, preferably, a previous employer, the Minister of a Church or a Civil Servant. And that's it!

Priscilla: Minister of a Church? Suppose I'm a Muslim?

1st Secretary: Well...you'll require a reference letter from your **thingy**, one from a previous employer or a civil servant.

Priscilla: *(Looks up at the ceiling for a while, and then, uninterestedly nods her head in approval).* I am interested in the post, but I can't have the interview today; I will do so tomorrow.

1st Secretary: That's entirely up to you. I would seize on this opportunity, if I were you. Vacancies don't sit by and wait for you, you see. *(She hands over a form to Priscilla).* Take a seat over there and complete this form; return it to me when you've finished. Good luck!

(She hands over the form to Priscilla, smiling at the same time) Well, I wish you the best of luck. *(She concentrates on entering some information into the computer. Presently, another secretary is available)*

2nd Secretary: Who's next please? *(Abou and Uche move over to the table. Abou offers the only seat to Uche; looks at both of them).* Who's first?

Abou: *(Tapping on Uche's shoulder)* He is. I am only here to assist him.

2nd Secretary: Right! I see... How can I help you, sir?

Uche: *(Looks over to Abou)* I am a university student looking for part-time work.

2nd Secretary: Very well, then. Ermm… Do you have any form of identification on you, sir?

Uche: Yes. *(He produces his passport and hands it over to the Secretary).*

2nd Secretary: Lovely! *(She flips through the pages of the passport).* Fantastic! Well, as you may be aware, the Home Office now permits International students to work for only 20 hours. You do need a National Insurance Number for a start.

Abou: We've obtained that from the Department of Social Security. *(To Uche)* You can show her the Temporary NI number that was given to you yesterday. *(Uche produces the Temporary NI slip and gives it to the Secretary).*

2nd Secretary: *(Examines the temporary NI slip)* Thanks. You do however need a permanent NI number after a month. What you need to do is, look at the advertised vacancies on the notice board and find out the ones that match your own interest and qualification.

Abou: We've already done that. *(To Uche)* Show her the list of vacancies we've identified!

Uche: *(Passes the form containing the vacancies to the 2nd secretary).*

2nd Secretary: *(She skims through)* Jolly good! Basically, what I'll have to do is, call the telephone numbers of the advertised positions. I must forewarn you that some of the vacancies advertised may be filled without our knowledge. So, it is possible for a post to be advertised with us here, while the position may have already been filled. Is that clear?

Uche: Okay.

2nd Secretary: Lovely. *(She dials and listens)* Oh! Hello! This is Helen at the Job Centre. I've Mr. *(She looks at Uche).*

Abou: Omotayo

2nd Secretary: *(Mispronounces the name. Abou and Uche exchange glances as she does so)* Mr. Ohmohmohta's here with me from the University. He wishes to apply for the post of Office Assistant in your Department. *(She listens)* Aha, okay, aright; I'll tell him. No problem. Thank you very much. Bye. *(She replaces the handset and turns to Uche)* I'm afraid, that post's no longer available. Shall we try the next one?

Uche: Yes!

2nd Secretary: Fingers crossed. *(She dials and listens).* Oh, hello. Is that *Safeway* Personnel Department? Great! This is Helen at the Job Centre. I've Mr. .. *(She looks at Uche again)*

Uche: Omotayo …

2nd Secretary: *(Mispronounces the name again. Abou and Uche glance at each other as she does so)* Ohmohtahyoo. He wishes to apply for the post of part-time security officer in your Department. *(She listens)* Aha. Aha. Hang on a sec. *(To Uche)* Have you ever worked as a security officer before?

Uche: *(Uncertain about what to say. He looks at Abou who nods in approval without even looking at Uche)* Yes!

2nd Secretary: The applicant has some experience… *(She listens)* Sorry? *(She listens)* Hang on. *(To Uche)* Can you fire a gun?

Uche: *(Uncertain)* Ye..es!

2nd Secretary: Yes, he can. *(She listens)* Right! Okay. Okay do. I'll tell him. That's fine. Thank you very much. Bye. *(The secretary turns to Uche)* Right! Ermm…, this one is a bit tricky. The vacancy's still available. However, the procedure is very demanding, I'm afraid. You'll be required to demonstrate that you can safely fire a short-gun at a specified target. Ermm…

Uche: *(Looks at Abou)*

Abou: Shall we try the other vacancy please?

2nd Secretary: Oh, certainly! *(She takes the handset again and dials. She listens)* Oh, hello! Is that the Personnel Department of the General Hospital? Lovely! I've a male student from the uni. He is interested in the post of porter/cleaner you advertised with us. *(She listens)* Aha! Fantastic! Okay do. Thank you very much. *(She turns to Uche and speaks with excitement)* The vacancy still exists, and the Personnel Department is very pleased to invite you for an interview tomorrow at 10.30 am! Would you like to take it?

Uche: *(Looks at Abou who nods in approval)* Yes please.

2nd Secretary: I thought so! Do you know your way to General Hospital?

Uche: No! But, my friend probably does. *(Looks at Abou for confirmation).*

Abou: *(He nods to indicate that he does).*

2nd Secretary: Fine; you're required to take along your passport, proof of National Insurance Number and names and addresses of three referees. One of the referees should be your most recent employer. *(She reaches out for a blank form that she hands over to Uche)* Please complete this form and return it to me when you are through. Okay?

Uche: Yes.

2nd Secretary: Good luck! Who's next please?

(The Secretaries and other characters on stage freeze as Abou and Uche take centre stage).

Uche: I can't understand that the only vacancies available are for menial jobs.

Abou: Fellow, in this country, you shouldn't be interested in the nature of the job on offer. The important thing is you're earning something from it.

Uche: *(After a while)* Maybe I should tell you that my wife is a secondary school teacher. Is it possible for her to get a teaching job?

Abou: Let's not worry about crossing a bridge before getting to it. I'm sure something will be worked out for your wife when she arrives.

Uche: Do you mean there is a possibility?

Abou: Only trained and qualified teachers from specified countries are allowed to teach in the UK. Even they are not automatically granted qualified teacher status (QTS). It means that if your wife wishes to work as a teacher, she will be required to pursue post-graduate diploma in education (PGDE).

Uche: Is the course free of charge?

Abou: *(He chuckles)* Free! Uche, let's take these things one at a time… I know a colleague whose wife used to be a secondary school teacher in Malawi. She is now a carer.

Uche: What work does a carer do?

Abou: Many people do not have the time to look after their parents at home, so they take them to Rest or Nursing homes and pay for the board, lodging and professional services of carers who look after their parents.

Uche: *(Surprised)* I see. I thought it was the government who pays …

Abou: Well, in some cases. Usually the residents, their children or relatives pay. That's why carers are paid good wages.

Uche: Really!

Abou: You'll be surprised to hear that a hard working carer can earn £500 - £1000!

Uche: *(Impressed)* You must be joking!

Abou: Look at this man! Some can earn even more than that.

Uche: Amazing! I should have chosen a caring job if you had told me this earlier.

Abou: Well, you may change your mind if you knew what caring entails...

Uche: Hmm. Anyway, caring may be suitable for my wife who is also interested in nursing.

Abou: Fortunately, your wife is a teacher not a nurse; you just said.

Uche: What are we going to do about the three referees?

Abou: You leave that to me. We should be going. I have an appointment with my supervisor at 3.00pm. Submit your form and let's be going.

(2nd Secretary and the other characters defreeze. Uche hands the completed form to the Secretary. Abou exits. All other characters exit, leaving Uche on stage. He walks to the centre of the stage, looks around and then at the audience. He looks confused.

Uche: *(Unimpressed)*Yeah... Is this the England I have heard and read about so much? Nah waa oo!

(Lights fade on stage).

End of scene

****

Act Two

Scene One

A Student's Private Life

(In this scene, Uche learns about the implications of immigration rules for spouses and children of international students. The setting is Eku's home. There are a separate living room, a dining room and three bedrooms. In the living room are a suite, TV and VCR, Hi-fi musical system and family pictures and certificates on the wall. National symbols such as flag, anthem, pledge and different currency notes are properly framed and placed on different sides of the wall. In the dining room are dining table, chairs, and a small refrigerator.

The family wake up to a busy schedule, cleaning, packing and then preparing lunch. Music of African origin can be heard in the background. Eku's wife, Marion, is a lively woman. She is appropriately dressed for the occasion, in wrapper and a female gown. The children - Martha, Amy, Marian and Marie are aged 18, 12, 9 and 5 respectively. They are casually dressed, in shorts and T-shirts. Their English is fluent. Marion and the two elder girls are busy in the kitchen, backstage. Eku is also casually dressed, in shorts and a short sleeve shirt. Marie, as always, is glued to the TV in the living room.

(Marion enters the dining room with clean hand-towels that she places in a drawer. On her way back to the kitchen, she notices Marie).

Marion: Marie!

Marie: Yes mum. *(She answers with little interest, concentrating on the TV).*

Marion: Honey, did you enjoy your breakfast? *(She moves to Marie and caresses her face).*

35

Marie: Not really, mum. (*She dodges her mother's hand, trying not to miss something on the TV screen*)

Marion: (*Surprised, she bends down to reach over Marie's ears*) Why not? But I thought bacon; sausages and beans are your favourites.

Marie: I prefer cornflakes today, mum. (*She smiles, trying to reassure her mother that everything is fine*).

Eku: (*Enters from backstage*) Yu go sahbi. Yu weit! Yu go no wehtha nah kohnflekes or kohl rehs yu go it foh brekfahs wen wi go tohn bahk nah wi kohntri. (*The comment in Krio sends the other children laughing backstage*)

Marie: What's that, dad?

Eku: I said we'd soon see whether you'd be asking for cornflakes or 'cold rice' in the morning, when we return home.

Marie: What's 'coldrice', dad? (*The term seems to draw her attention away from the TV and she is seen to be interested in getting an explanation from her father*)

Eku: It's leftover food that is heated up in the morning.

Marie: Oh, leftover! I don't like leftovers, dad.

(*Marion forgets returning to the kitchen for a while and listens to the interesting conversation between Eku and Marie. Marian and Martha also walk into the living room to join in*)

Marian: But leftovers aren't bad. We do eat leftovers even here.

Marie: No, we don't!

Amy: Yes, we do. The sauce we ate yesterday was a leftover from two days ago.

Martha: *(Getting agitated)* No, it wasn't. Mum cooked that sauce and kept it specifically for two days. That's not a leftover. Was it, mum?

Marion: That's not what you call a leftover. Marie! Leftovers aren't bad, as long as they are properly preserved. *(She retires to the kitchen).*

Eku: Marie, nobody would eat leftovers if they were harmful…

Marie: *(Unconvinced)* Thanks dad *(She resumes watching the TV programme).*

(Marion exits to backstage. Eku increases the volume of music that gradually fills the air. Presently, the guests arrive - Ibrahim, Maama, his spouse, their son, Ansu, and Uche. Each of the guests, with the exception of Ansu, is dressed in typical African attire. Ibrahim's wife, Maama, is more outspoken and outgoing. Eku welcomes the elder guests).

Marie: *(Joins her father at the door to welcome Ansu)* Hi Ansu. Come on Ansu, come! Come and see! *(She leads Ansu through the curtains to back of the stage)*

(Eku leads Ibrahim, Maama and Uche into the living room, situated at the centre of the stage. Eku reduces the volume of the music, as the guests sit and settle down to drink and chat).

Uche: Oga, this is a big house.

Eku: Well, by this country's standard, a three-bedroom house is a big house. But, you know what a big house in Nigeria or Sierra Leone looks like.

Uche: Ah, Oga! I will be mad to compare houses in this country to the ones we have at home. I was thinking of my grave-like room at the student hostel when I made that comment.

Ibrahim: Houses and bedrooms in this country are generally very small; space on this island is a big problem. Notice the narrow roads, narrow parking spaces, small houses and bedrooms.

Eku: Yet, the rent is so expensive! We are paying £570.00 per month, excluding water rate, electricity bills and the cost of other utilities!

Uche: *(shocked)* My God!

Ibrahim: Most students with families of the size of Eku's spend no less than that amount on housing alone!

Maama: We live in a studio flat - two bedrooms, a living room, kitchen and bathroom. And we pay £300.00 per month!

Uche: That amount is sufficient for renting a mansion in Lagos!

(Presently, Marion emerges from the kitchen. She observes the usual courtesies, shaking hands with the male visitors and hugging Maama).

Marion: How is the nursing course?

Maama: Fine, my sister. You know all about adult education for an African lady in this country, a bit of schoolwork here, a bit of domestic work there and some agency work for the Queen's head.

Marion: My sister, that's the 21st century form of slavery. And this time, the masters are not flogging and binding us in chains, we actually come begging to be misused...

Maama: And abused…

(While the elders are chatting, Martha and her younger sisters prepare the dinner table at one end of the stage centre. The table and chairs for 10 is laid. The food, plates, cutlery, towels, drinks and cups are all placed accordingly. Martha, the eldest girl, advances towards her mother to inform her that dinner is served)

Martha: Mum, we've finished

Marion: Eku, IB, Uche and Maama, dinner is served.

Eku: *(To the guests)* Dinner is ready. Please take your drinks with you into the dining room. Where is Ansu?

Maama: I think he is with Marie in her room upstairs.

Eku: *(Calls out louder)* Marie! Ansu!

Ansu: *(The children answer from backstage)* Here uncle.

Marie: Yes dad.

Maama: It's time to eat something and then continue to play.

(Ansu and Martha enter from backstage, running towards Maama into the dining room)

Ansu and Marie: *(simultaneously)* I first.

Maama: Careful! Or you lose your teeth before dinner.

(Eku and the other guests move towards the dining table and take their seats in order. Martha, Amy and Marian join the rest from the kitchen. Before they start to dish up).

Eku: IB, bless this gift.

Ibrahim: Let's pray. *(They all close their eyes)* Lord, we thank you for this gift that we are about to eat. We thank you, O Lord, that we can afford and consume it. Lord, help those who have but cannot eat, and those who can eat, but do not have. Bless this home, O Lord, and the African communities at home and abroad. Grant us the wisdom to recognise and accept our mistakes. Lord, continue to provide us with the gifts of life. For all these and more, we pray in the name of Jesus Christ our Lord, from whom all good things come. Amen.

All: Amen.

Eku: Thank you, IB. Well, eat or you starve!

(The elder guests and hosts respectively, take their share of the food, as appropriate. Maama dishes out for Ansu, as Marion does the same for Marie. Eku demands a bowl of water to wash his hands, which is provided. The low African music in the background adds to the ambience).

Uche: *(Even before he starts to eat)* Ah! Ah! Chief! This is like an African restaurant; the aroma is tantalizing. Where do you buy these exotic African food varieties?

Eku: We occasionally do our food shopping in London, at Brixton or Peckham markets. There, you can get everything, from palm oil to bush-meat.

Uche: *(Impressed)* Hmm. I see! Madam, if you grant me permission, I fit eat with my hand, as we go do in my kohntri.

Marion: Why not!

Marie: *(Tries to attract her mother's attention)* Mummy, why does dad eat <u>foofoo</u> with his hands?

Marion: *(Smiling and tantalisingly looking at Eku)* You may ask him.

Marie: *(Curiously)* Dad, why do you eat <u>foofoo</u> with your hands?

Eku: I enjoy eating with my hands because one handful is equal to one mouthful. It will take two to three spoonfuls to fill my big mouth, you know, so I don't like eating with a spoon when I am hungry.

Marie: *(Unconvinced)* I don't like eating with my hands, dad. You can get your hands doh'ee. And, you can see' doh'ee bits in your fingernails. That's 'yuck'.

Maama: *(Patiently)* Marie, show me your right hand!

(Marie shows out her right hand to Maama. Everyone pays attention as Maama educates Marie on the use of hands.)

Maama: Now, let's spell the word spoon by counting the fingers on your right hand. *(Spelling and counting her fingers at the same time)* S-p-o-o-n. So you see! Our hands are also like spoons that we use.

Marie and Ansu: *(Ecstatically celebrate)* Yippy!

(After a brief while)

Uche: Hmm! The <u>foofoo</u> is fresh and the okra sauce is extremely delicious!

Ibrahim: Madam, you should apply to a four star hotel. What's your problem? You cook better than some of these chefs who appear on TV the whole day.

Maama: Will 'they' employ her?

Marian: Don't mind IB. He knows that certain kinds of jobs in this country are for certain people.

Ibrahim: *(He chuckles and tries to change the subject. To the elder girls)* Which of you helped mum to prepare the meal?

Amy: I cooked the okra-sauce for the <u>foofoo</u>, and also boiled the '<u>veggies</u>'.

Martha: *(Eagerly)* I washed the dishes and pots after cooking.

Marion: All of them can cook, except the youngest two.

Marian: Mum, I can cook.

Marion: Honey, I know you can.

Maama: *(Referring to Marian)* Can you cook all types of food?

Marian: Naaaa.

Maama: I imagine that the elder girls learnt to cook before they came to the UK. Back home, more opportunities exist for children to learn how to cook. Here, I can see that the opportunities are for eating pre-cooked foods, such as Kentucky Fried Chicken, McDonalds and Burger King.

Eku: What do you expect? Children learn these skills from their parents. If mum doesn't know how to cook, the son or daughter may not learn from them.

(They finish eating their share of food. Eku, Ibrahim and Uche wash their hands with soap, in water that Marian provides for them. They wipe their hands with towels already available for each person. Uche takes the lead in expressing appreciation for the dinner).

Uche: Oga, Marion and the girls, thank you very much for this delicious meal. When I go home, I will call Fatou and inform her that I have eaten cassava leaf sauce and home grown rice in the heart of England!

Eku and Marion: It's our pleasure.

Maama: Eku, thank you. Marion and the girls, thank you very much for the hospitality. The food is very Yummy.

Eku and Marion: Please don't mention.

Ibrahim: Madam, the chief himself and you, my children, thank you for the kind reception and the yummy lunch. As our people say, 'May you accumulate more to replace what we've consumed'?

Eku and Marion: Not at all.

Ansu: Thank you, 'uncle'. Thank you, 'aunty'.

Martha: Thanks, mummy. Thanks, daddy.

Eku and Marion: *(They acknowledge the appreciation by the children)*

(Parents and younger children exit from the stage. The elder girls clear the dining table and also exit. Lights fade)

End of Scene

Act Two

Scene Two

The Same

Implications of Visa Restrictions

(Marie and Ansu enter and occupy one end of stage. They mime the action of playing children's games. The elder daughters join them, and also mime the action of playing a board game. The parents and Uche re-enter the living room, situated at stage centre. They chat, watch a TV programme and drink at the same time).

Maama: *(Pensively examines the elder girls at play)* Time flies; these children are growing so well. *(To Marion)* How long have they lived in England for?

Marion: December 23rd 1998 will make them exactly two years old in the UK. *(Marion takes one of the family albums from under the coffee table and passes it on to Maama).* This photo album contains their pictures during the first week of arrival in the UK.

Maama: *(As she flips through the photographs)* Look at Marie! *(To Marion)* Was this at the airport?

Marion: *(She peers into the album)* Yes! That was at Gatwick Airport.

(Maama passes the album to Uche, who also looks through it. As he does so).

Uche: Oh! So, you did not travel together with the children?

Eku: No! We were reunited with these girls almost a year after my arrival in the UK. It's a long story, my brother.

Uche: Hmmm.

(By this time, Uche is no longer looking at the pictures, but attentively listening to the narrative. The rest of the other elders give audience to, or participate in the account of the children's journey from Africa to the UK)

Eku: When I got this scholarship, Sierra Leone's war was not yet over. However, after the elections in 1996 that brought President Kabba to power, conditions appeared to have been returning to normal...

Marion: By the time he left, on September 20th 1996, schools and colleges were functioning relatively well, especially in the capital. All four of our children were very well settled in some of the best primary and secondary schools in Freetown. His cousin and wife *(Indicating the picture of the couple on the wall)* accepted to accommodate and look after our children during the period of his study in the UK.

Eku: The original plan was that Marion would accompany me in December of that year, so that she could improve her educational standard, as well as helping with some household chores.

Marion: *(Intrusively)* He can't even boil an egg.

(Maama giggles, while Uche and Ibrahim remain unmoved by the comment)

Eku: That went according to plan, except that Marion arrived later than we had hoped.

Uche: Well, thank God for that. At least the British High Commission in Freetown did not treat you as they did Abou and his wife in Banjul.

Marion: In actual fact, it did not go as smoothly as Eku has explained. For example, we were forced into obtaining separate passports for each of the children. Originally, the names of all four children were on my own passport; that complicated my own application for the UK visa.

Ibrahim: Of course, stamping the visa into your passport implied granting all the other names included in it.

Marion: IB, first of all, the Consular officer wanted to confirm that the children were all ours…

Uche: *(Surprised)* Really!

Eku: Oh yes! Marion says that the Consular Officer was a very young ginger-haired boy who treated people like filth.

Uche: That's their habit

Marion: At one stage, I really ran out of patience…

(Marion gazes blankly at the children. As she does so, lights fade on the characters on stage. When it resumes, Marion is in a long queue. The people in the queue joke or complain about the foolhardiness of the current Consular Officer at the British High Commission).

1st Client: *(Surprised)* Marion! So, you haven't gone to England yet!

Marion: How could I, my sister?

1st Client: *(Amazed)* I thought 'the devil' had left you off the hook.

Marion: The man is a real 'devil'! The last time he sent to call me it was to ask for the children's birth certificates.

2nd Client: And you produced them?

Marion: Yes. Then he said, 'We will keep in touch with you'.

1st Client: In that case, you're luckier; he did not stamp your passport as he did Fatima's. It is worse to have your passport stamped after refusing to grant you visa. If you are refused visa once, you can only apply for it after 5 years!

2nd Client: Is your passport still at the High Commission?

Marion: Yes.

2nd Client: Then, you should be hopeful.

3rd Client: My sister, you shouldn't worry yourself. Your application is very straightforward. Your husband is on a full-time course on a prestigious scholarship. 'The devil' will waste your time but in the end, he will grant you the visa. It's people like us who have been invited on a visit that should be worried. The Consular Officer will think that we are going to their country to claim asylum.

1st Client: Do you blame them for treating us like this? Aren't our brothers and sisters claiming asylum everyday all over Europe? We are ourselves to blame for the insolence we suffer in the hands of immigration officials.

(There is a brief spell of silence)

Marion: *(Breaking the silence)* This new officer is very unpredictable. I have heard that he refused to grant visa even to spouses of students who have scholarship and on a full-time courses!

1st Client: I don't know about that...

2nd Client: The truth is that the High Commission is turning down lots of applications at present. Last month, a child whose parents already reside in the UK was refused entry clearance.

Marion: My God! Does it mean that the British High Commission has become more difficult than the American Embassy?

1st Client: How dare you compare the American Embassy to the British High Commission! At the American Embassy, visa applicants start queuing up from midnight onwards! And the office normally closes before 12.00 noon, interviewing not more than 10 people per day!

(Presently, a voice from back stage calls out, 'Mrs Marion Scotland')

Marion: Yes please!

(Marion moves across the stage. She occupies a seat in front of a table; behind it is seated a ginger-haired, lean, hungry looking and casually dressed gentleman. On the table is a folder. The gentleman welcomes Marion, holding a piece of paper in his hand)

Consular Officer: Good morning, Mrs. Scotland.

Marion: Good morning sir.

Consular Officer: *(Sarcastically)* I haven't been knighted yet. Call me Shaun.

Marion: Pardon me, sir.

Consular Officer: *(He makes faces)* Never mind. Now! Where were we?

Marion: Sir!

Consular Officer: *(Ignoring her)* Now, Mrs. Scotland, this is not your visa interview. I have invited you to carry out some preliminary investigations. To start with, I should tell you that I have received your children's birth certificates. They are fine!

Marion: Okay, sir.

Consular Officer: *(He makes faces)* So, are all the four girls the children of you and Mr. Scotland?

Marion: Yes!

Consular Officer: You must have been very young by the time you had your first daughter…

Marion: Sir!

Consular Officer: *(He makes faces again)* Your children's dates of birth?

Marion: They are on the certificates, sir.

Consular Officer: *(He makes faces again)* I know, but I want you to tell me.

Marion: *(Looks bewildered)*

Consular Officer: Okay, Mrs. Scotland. Who is going to look after your children in the absence of you and your husband?

Marion: My husband's brother will look after them.

Consular Officer: *(Curiously)* Why are you so certain that your husband's brother will care for your children properly?

Marion: In our culture, our relatives take good care of our children, sometimes, in much the same way as the parents themselves do, if not even better.

Consular Officer: Do you hope to be reunited with your children in due course?

Marion: My husband will decide.

Consular Officer: *(Very surprised)* Why not you?

Marion: He has the final say.

Consular Officer: *(Shocked)* Really! *(After a long pause)* What are you going to do in the UK?

Marion: My husband has invited me to join him.

Consular Officer: *(Impatiently)* I know that. The question is, "What are you going to do there?"

Marion: I'm going to join my husband.

Consular Officer: *(Recognising her recalcitrance)* How long do you hope to stay in the UK for?

Marion: My husband has explained it in the invitation letter that I submitted with my application form.

Consular Officer: *(Getting more impatient)* What was your husband's job before he left for his studies, Mrs. Scotland?

Marion: My husband was a lecturer in the University.

Consular Officer: Right! Mrs. Scotland, I'm afraid that you may not be able to join your husband before Christmas. We will contact you as soon as we are satisfied that it is okay to grant you leave to remain in the UK.

Marion: Yes, sir.

Consular Officer: *(He makes faces)* See you soon.

(Lights fade on Marion and the Consular Officer. A while later, the lights resume on the home setting of Eku's family in the UK. The characters take their respective places and resume activities on stage)

Uche: It must have been an ordeal for you…

Ibrahim: It's also true that some of the immigration officers are either very inexperienced or naturally callous!

Maama: 'Callous' is the word!

Eku: Anyway, as I was saying, Marion's visa didn't cause us much problem as the children's. The original plan was to bring Marian and Marie. This was not going to happen until I had returned home for my PhD fieldwork. Unfortunately, on Saturday, the 25th of May 1997, disaster struck!

Uche: *(Anxiously)* What happened?

Marion: The elected government was overthrown by the military regime, known as Armed Forces Revolutionary Council (AFRC). That military coup threw all our plans into the air.

Uche: Oh! I remember those soldiers. That was the regime that Sani Abacha helped President Kabba to uproot.

Maama: You should have seen Eku and Marion at that time.

Eku: My brother! I could neither eat nor sleep well.

Marion: *(Indicating)* Those children have lived through nightmares.

Uche: I know exactly what war means for children at that age. Two of my childhood years were spent during the Biafra war in Nigeria *(He shakes his head)* May God forbid me from such experiences again!

(There is a grim silence).

Eku: *(Breaking the silence)* At the end of the day, it was only through the grace of God almighty that we were able to bring those children to safety. But this lady *(he gets up and takes a picture of a retired English lady from the wall)* was the God sent saviour. She made it all possible. *(Alluding to the photograph)* We owe you depths of gratitude, Ann. Where ever you are today, and may God forever reward you for your loving care and unflinching support.

Marion: Some people would have told you that the British are generally cold, indifferent and insensitive people. But, that's an unguarded over-generalisation.

Eku: As the situation at home worsened, Marion convinced me to discuss the matter with the *Students Advice and Welfare Centre*. It was at that Centre I met this God sent saviour. Oh! Ann is like an angel on earth. Her professionalism is second to none that I know of. Her immediate reactions to my story were so comforting, soothing and reassuring that I was forced into rethinking my prejudices about British people.

Marion: *(Referring to Ann's photograph)* Ann did not only provide advice and information, she even championed the cause of bringing our children to safety. She didn't stop at that, Ann has gone out of her way to seek all kinds of support and assistance for us; that has made all the difference to our lives in the UK. She is a mother to my husband and myself and a grandmother to our children.

Ibrahim: My brother, all is not lost. There are still a few good people on earth…

Marion: The solicitor we hired for the children's visas was sharp and very efficient. I remember the letter she wrote to the British High Commissioner in Banjul.

Eku: That was a cracker! It was after the Consular Officer demanded DNA tests from us for our four children. In the first place, the cost of this test was prohibitive for us. Moreover, the DNA test was going to stall the entire application process. You then wonder why the High Commission required marriage and birth certificates in the first place. Thanks to God and for that strongly worded letter, our children would have been languishing in Banjul by now.

(After a brief while)

Maama: I never knew about these fine details of your children's travel. Did you perform this DNA test, after all the hassle?

Marion: No! Less than 24 hours after the letter, we received a fax informing us that our children's visas have been processed.

Uche: Dis wan full my mouth like dry garri!

Marion: Remember that even with the help of the solicitor, we had to fulfil all the requirements of the application: contract for our accommodation, proof of sufficient funds to maintain the children after their arrival, our marriage and birth certificates, and the children's own birth certificates, supporting letters from the member of Parliament of our constituency, letters from the

Minister of our church, supervisor and sponsors. It was a very involving adventure.

Uche: <u>Wa-ha-la! Nah wetin bi dis</u>?

Maama: Oh yes!

Eku: Let no one deceive you, applying for UK visa is real wahala.

Ansu: *(He is running towards his mum away from Marie)* Mummy! Mummy!

Maama: Ansu, careful! *(She grabs Ansu)* Marie! Why is this young man running away from you?

Marie: He smacked me and then ran away.

Ansu: She took my *Pokemon* cards, mummy.

Maama: And, what did you do?

Marie: He was 'taking the Mick'…

Ansu: I didn't do that, mummy.

Marie: Yes! You did!

Ibrahim: Ansu, you don't court a woman with violence.

Eku: Yes, IB. How do you do it?

(They laugh about it)

Maama: *(To Ansu)* Go on! What do you say to someone when you hurt him or her?

Ansu: Sorry, Marie.

Marie: That's okay.

Maama: *(To both of them)* You may go and play with your *Pokemon* cards *(Ansu and Marie dash away through the curtains to back of the stage)*.

Uche: Ah! Children…

Marion: Once they are together, they never get tired of offending and reporting.

Eku: It's like the kitchen knife and the cook, they do get along well but sometimes they disagree.

Ibrahim: *(Trying to change the subject again. To Uche)* My brother, stories about the mistreatments we have suffered due to immigration rules are numerous.

Eku: Ah! Ibrahim's own experience was a unique one. I always get angry when I think about the frustration and embarrassment we suffered on that fateful day.

Uche: Hmmm!

Ibrahim:*(To Uche)* In my own case, I obtained the air ticket and visa for my spouse before leaving Nigeria. However, we couldn't travel together because Maama was critically pregnant. Our parents thought that it was advisable for her to deliver her first baby at home.

Maama: You know the advantages…

Ibrahim: Fortunately, she gave birth successfully to a baby boy, three days after my departure. Because she already had the ticket and visa, we decided that she could travel when the child was one month old. Little did we know that a one-month old child is really old enough to require leave to remain in UK.

Uche: You must be joking!

Eku: Joking!

Maama: My own travel overseas was not a quiet event. The farewell party involved the whole village and neighbouring communities. It was a memorable party. There was plenty of food, ecstatic masquerade dancing. It was a typical African send-off for the daughter of a well-to-do village headman...

(Presently, Maama gazes at the ceiling to conceal her tears, shaking her head in despair. She squeezes both eyes, stopping her tears from rolling down her cheek. She is lost in imagination. Lights fade out on her, as the sound of drumming could be heard in the background. A while later, the lights brighten on drummers, singers and different masquerades that appear on stage in order of their importance. The drumming gets frantic, amidst the exotic noises of the masquerades and their conductors. An entourage led by a well-dressed middle-aged man enter from the opposite end of the stage. A young boy places a chair at the stage centre. The chair is then neatly covered by a piece of white cloth. The middle-aged man who leads the entourage mounts the chair and faces the masquerades and the crowd, the latter presently absorbed by the music).

Young man: *(Speaks in Yoruba)* Ehdakeh! Ehdakeh! *(The drumming and singing dies down. Almost immediately, there is astonishing silence).* The chief wants to speak!

Pa Ayoka: My people! I say thanks to you all. As our elders say, one tree cannot make a forest as one person cannot make a crowd. Without you, this celebration would be impossible. We needed people to eat the food we have cooked, to drink the palm wine we have provided, to dance to the rhythms of the *Shehgbuleh*, the drums and other musical instruments. That is why I thank you all on behalf of my family. *(He clears his throat)* You all know why we have assembled here today. In case you don't, we have gathered here to say farewell to my eldest daughter, Maama, who will be travelling to the white man's country to join her husband. Let me at this point call on Alhaji Moidawu to lead us in Islamic prayers.

Alhaji: Al Fatiha *(Surah Al- Fatiha is recited. Alhaji recites a few verses from the holy Qur'an. He ends with prayers and blessings for Maama, including wishing her safe journey and success during her stay).*

Pa Ayoka: Thank you Alhaji. We will also call on pastor Jakka to lead us in Christian prayers.

Pastor: The Lord's Prayer. *(The prayer is recited by members of the crowd that could. Pastor then prays for Maama, for her parents, relatives and for everybody).*

Pa Ayoka: We must always thank God for everything. He gives us life and has made it possible for us to be here today. May that God guide and protect us from harm and danger, particularly on this occasion. Among our people, you don't stop a dance for long speeches without showing your worth *(Thumping his chest).* We show our worth with money! And, as long as the coffee and cacao trees are bearing fruits, I will never know poverty. *(He dips his right hand into his trousers pocket and reaches out for a bundle of bank notes, which he takes out and arrogantly displays. Instructing the musicians)* Oni lu eh behreh.

(Presently, the drumming and singing resumes. Father feigns the action of lavishing money on each of the masquerades, drummers and singers. Each masquerade performs its best steps as its conductor receives some local currency notes on its behalf. After a while, the head woman comes and hangs head with Father. He orders the activities to halt for a second time).

Pa Ayoka: The time has come for the real thing. I now invite each one of you to the chief's compound.

(Father then leads the procession out of stage in jubilant and ecstatic mood. Moments later, Father, Maama and other close family members re-appear on stage. They sit in a semi-circle, with Maama at the centre. Father breaks the silence).

Pa Ayoka: Family members, we have come to the private part of this farewell ceremony. It is now time to pray for our child. We will begin with Musu who is the mother. Pray for this, your only daughter.

Sisi Ada: If prayers alone can fill someone's stomach, Maama would be constipated by now. *(To Maama)* My dear child, give me your right hand! *(Maama stretches out her hand. Mother then blows out some saliva onto it and instructs her to put it on her forehead. She does so).* You have my blessings. As long as I have lived all my life obeying your father, then no harm will come your way during your stay overseas. Our prayers and blessings will serve as a shield to protect you in anything you will do. Go and prosper, and bring us more grandchildren.

All: Amen

Pa Ayoka: Uncle! You will pray next.

Pa Oni: My sister has said everything. Maama, give me your right hand. *(Maama stretches out her hand. Uncle spits some saliva onto it and instructs her to put the hand on her forehead. She does).* You're our sweat and blood. Our people have taught us to believe that when the mother slavishly endures the wrath of marriage, her offspring will reap the benefit. May you therefore reap the reward for all that my sister is enduring in her own marriage.

All: Amen.

Pa Oni: May you take after your mother's footsteps. For a woman, obedience is the key to every successful marriage. Do not be carried away by the attractions of the new world. You're our only hope. May God go with you, and may he guide you in all your undertakings.

All: Amen.

Pa Ayoka: Thank you very much, uncle. Let me clarify one point. Your sister is not a slave in this household. She is obedient; and, as you can see, an occasion like this is the reward for that obedience. Maama, I have only one thing to add to what your mother and uncle have said. We are not sending you abroad to come back tomorrow with problems. You are not blind. You have seen what the children of Alhaji in America are doing for him. They have built and furnished that big mansion *(indicating)*. They have bought a Mercedes Benz car and are always sending money for Alhaji and his wives. I don't expect any less from you and your husband. You have never failed me in all your life. So, don't fail me this time. May God go with you... Al-fatiha! *(They recite surah Al-Fatiha)*. The Lords Prayer! *(They also recite the Lord's Prayer)*. Thank you all for coming. *(To Maama)*. You can now leave and attend to your child, and don't sleep very late!

(Light fades on Father and the other relatives, and brightens on Maama, Ibrahim and others in Eku's living room).

Maama: ...It was a lavish and befitting occasion. And so, the following day, I departed via Egypt Airlines. The trouble started in Cairo.

Uche: *(Impatiently)* Hmmmm.

Maama: As you would expect, the Egyptian Airline transited in Cairo to refuel or pick more passengers. Barely 30 minutes into the transit, I had an announcement in the public address system, requesting me to report immediately to the receptionist. There was an air of urgency about the announcement that made my heart jump. Carrying the one-month old child on my shoulder, I hurried to the receptionist. "I am Maama Ibrahim Onike", I announced myself to the receptionist, who then told me that my baby and I would not proceed on the journey to London Heathrow.

Uche: *(Curiously)* Why?

Maama: Because our one-month old son did not have leave to remain in the UK! "But my husband holds a Commonwealth Scholarship and is currently at the airport waiting to receive us." I pleaded. "You don't understand. If this aeroplane transports an illegal immigrant into the UK, our Airline will be fined the sum of £2000", the official explained. "The best we can do is to arrange a return flight for you and your son to Lagos", he said.

Uche: Unbelievable!

Ibrahim: Meanwhile, good friends like Eku, Abou and myself had hired a van bought plenty of drinks and food and travelled to London Heathrow airport. We were one hour early, since we did not want to take any chances. As soon as we arrived, we took our places in front of the big screen.

Eku: You remember the TV screens at the airport that indicate flight schedules? Our eyes were all glued on one of those screens, looking at the flight number of the plane that Maama and Ansu were expected to arrive in. The plane was about 30 minutes late, arriving at 8.00pm.

Ibrahim: Barely thirty minutes after it had touched down, we could hear my name being announced over the public address system. "Will Mr. Ibrahim Onike, who is expecting Maama

Ibrahim Onike from Lagos, report to the reception please!" Several thoughts raced through my mind. "What could have happened to my child during the journey?" I pondered as I went to the receptionist. When the news was broken to me, I was dumbfounded for a start. And then, it dawned on me that my wife and young child were stranded in a no man's land, without adequate money or requirements for proper childcare!

Uche: *(Shocked)* My God!

Ibrahim: "Where is my wife and child, and how could I contact them?" I asked in desperation. In a professional manner, an airline official narrated the full story to me. You can imagine how we all felt.

Eku: Fellow! Let that day never come again.

Maama: Fortunately, by the time we arrived at Murtalla Mohammed airport, Ibrahim's brothers were already waiting to receive us.

Eku: Stories about the consequences of immigration rules are unending…

Uche: It's a real blessing to have met people like you. I have learnt so much during this short period of my arrival in the UK.

(After a long pause)

Ibrahim: The Chief himself! We must leave you so that you can have some rest.

Maama: Martha, when will you be free to plait my hair again?

Marian: Next weekend, 'aunty'.

Maama: That's fine for me. When should I pick you up?

Marian: (*Looking to her mum*) Mum, when will aunty...

Marion: On Saturday, after 10.00 am.

Maama: Fine. Thank you, Marion. Girls! I will see you again on Saturday.

Ibrahim: Eku, there is something I must tell you. As you know, our visas have already expired. I have applied for a year's extension to enable Maama complete her nursing course. I am not expecting any problems, but with the Home Office, you can't be sure of anything.

Eku: Let's leave it to God almighty. He works in mysterious ways, his wonders to perform. We will lift you in our prayers from now on.

Ibrahim: Thank you, my brother. We need prayers more than anything else at this time. *(To Marion and the girls)* Marion and the girls, thank you very much for the sumptuous meal and for the company. *(To Uche)* We could give you a lift.

Uche: Oh! Thanks for the offer. *(Shaking hands with Eku and alternates between formal English and Pidgin)* Thank you very much for your warm hospitality. Madam, I beg, thanks you for everything. I have enjoyed every minute of my stay. Girls, thank you for the food. I will keep in touch. *(They observe the usual courtesies of parting).*

End of Scene

****

Act Two

Scene Three

At Priscilla and Kisa's home

The setting is the home of Priscilla and her husband, Kisa. Kisa is a soft spoken and unassuming gentleman. He is wearing shorts and a T-Shirt that bears the slogan: 'Power to women'. Presently, Kisa is miming the action of doing the household chores - dishwashing, hovering the living room, dusting the furniture and electrical appliances, drying the washing and washing the pots. He hums one of Peter Tosh's tunes: 'Equal rights and justice', as he does so. As he starts preparing the condiments for cooking their dinner, Uche arrives and presses the doorbell. Kisa leaves the preparation to open the door)

Kisa: Who's it?

Uche: Ah! Chief nah me, Uche.

Kisa: *(Welcomes Uche)* Ah! Bwana, jambo.

Uche: Oga how you de? *(They both realise they cannot speak each other's Pidgin and Swahili respectively.)*

Kisa: How are you, Uche?

Uche: Oga, I'm fine, trying to find a foothold in this new culture.

Kisa: *(He chuckles)* A drink?

Uche: Yes, please.

Kisa: Tea, coffee, beer?

Uche: Oga, I can't deny beer from you. What brands do you have?

63

Kisa: *Carling* and *Stella Artois.*

Uche: I prefer *Stella Artois.*

Kisa: *(Goes backstage and re-appears with a can of beer and a glass. He hands them to Uche. Uche opens the drink, ignores the glass and takes a swig from the can).* I was doing some work when you came in.

Uche: Oh! Then, I'm sorry to interrupt you. Priscilla has agreed to lend me her copy of a text on research methodology. She gave me this note for you. *(Hands the note over to Kisa)*

Kisa: *(Skims through the note, smiling as he does so. He mutters)* Ah Priscilla...

Uche: Sorry!

Kisa: No, I was talking to myself. My wife is expecting the food to be ready by mid-day. She is very hungry and is tired of eating at the SU refectory.

Uche: *(Shocked)* Excuse me, <u>Oga</u>. Do you cook for your wife?

Kisa: Yep! In fact, I don't only cook; I also do the other household chores so that she can do her studies in peace. Why do you ask?

Uche: *(He laughs hysterically. He savagely gulps the beer from the can and places the empty can on the table)* <u>Please, I beg,</u> give me another can. *(Kisa retires to the back of the stage to fetch another beer.)* My God! Cook for my own wife!

(Kisa returns with another can of beer and a soft drink for himself. He gives the beer to Uche and opens the soft drink for himself. They sit and begin to chat)

Uche: So, you are the cook!

Kisa: Actually, I take care of the home to enable Priscilla to concentrate on her studies.

Uche: I see! How do you feel, doing Priscilla's own work for her?

Kisa: *(He sniggers)* I used to think like you. Honestly! I used to feel the same way.

Uche: *(Bewildered)* So, why the sudden change?

Kisa: I have realised that I was making unfair demands on Priscilla.

Uche: What do you mean, 'unfair demands'? It's a woman's job to give birth to children, cook meals, perform the household chores, and what have you.

Kisa: *(Calmly)* And the man's job is…?

Uche: *(Ponders for a while)* Look at this man! *(Proudly)* The -- man – is -- the --- bread -- winner!

Kisa: But, women too can be breadwinners. Here, in this country, Priscilla is the breadwinner. Is there anything wrong with that?

Uche: *(Sobers up, but still agitated)* Don't tell me you're not working!

Kisa: Of course, I am! But the wages I earn from distributing mails is nowhere near my wife's stipend and allowances. As a result, she prefers that we live on her income, and I do whatever I choose with the pennies I receive from Royal Mail.

Uche: Hmmmm. Well...My friend, whether my income is a penny or not, I don't see myself allowing my wife to rule my household.

Kisa: Uche, you are confusing matters. I have not said that because Priscilla provides our daily bread, she rules this household all by herself. Far from it! On the contrary, we take decisions based on consensus. I think that is a fairer way of running a home.

Uche: My brother, our parents did not teach us to run our homes in this way.

Kisa: *(Amused)* Ah! That's exactly the view I contest. In today's world, we should learn to adjust and adapt our lives to our present circumstances. And if this means we should do things that our parents did not do, then, so be it *(He takes a sip from his can)*.

Uche: I can see that life in this part of the world really warps people's mentality. Eh! Is it because of the influence of the TV?

Kisa: Fellow, this has nothing to do with the West or TV. It's plain commonsense. As our people say, "'Thank you' is a short nice phrase. Everyone knows and would like to say it to the other. No one should claim monopoly over it'. Like us, our women are human. They are not slaves. We should learn to treat them with dignity and respect.

Uche: *(He looks up at the ceiling with open hands, as if to conjure)* Jesus Christ, kohm and hear dis! Kisa, how long have you been married to Priscilla?

Kisa: 5 years ago. Why?

Uche: *(He takes a swig from his can of beer and wipes his mouth)* Why have you learnt these salient views on matrimony only now, here, in England?

Kisa: *(Being sarcastic)* Because I have. I'm saying to you, it's never too late for you to learn as well… *(He sniffs around and exclaims)* Oh! Excuse me... I've left that pot unattended *(He dashes off stage)*

Uche: *(After a brief silence. Appears to be pensive.)* Actually, Kisa has a point. *(Pauses)* But, me, Uche, cook! … Hmmmm… Thank God, I don't even know how to …

Light fades

End of Scene

****

Denouement
(Six Months later)

(The setting is the living room of Eku and family. It is almost past midnight, the clock on the wall should indicate this when the lights resume. It is pitch dark. Eku and family are presumably asleep, backstage. There is perfect silence. Moments later, the telephone rings. After ringing for the third time, the voice of Marion, Eku's wife, could be heard, trying to wake Eku up from his slumber).

Marion: Eku! Eku!

Eku: Hmm.

Marion: Eku!

Eku: Hmmm! What?

Marion: It's the phone. Can't you hear it? *(The phone continues to ring for another minute).*

Eku: Who is calling at this time of day?

(As Eku enters the living room to answer the call, the stage lights brighten up. He looks at the wall clock to confirm the time of day as he lifts the handset to answer the telephone. He does so apprehensively)

Eku: *(In low tones)* Hello. Hello. *(He listens attentively)* IB? Is that you? *(He listens)* Wha.. What is it?

(Presently, Marion inches her way into the living room to join Eku)

Marion: *(Curiously whispering)* Who is it?

Eku: *(Continues to listen as he indicates to Marion to stay still)* My God! Oh No! *(Pauses for a while)* Do you want us to come over? Or.. *(He listens)* Okay. We look forward to seeing you.

Eku: *(He replaces the handset, sinks into the sofa and heaves a huge sigh of despair)* Oh my God!

Marion: Who was it?

Eku: Ibrahim

Marion: What is it?

Eku: They're just returning from a trek and they have received an awful letter from the Home Office. *(He heaves another sigh)*

Marion: How awful?

Eku: You like asking unnecessary questions …

Marion: Eku! Why do you talk as if I have already read through the letter the Home Office has written to IB and his family?

Eku: *(Unnecessarily losing his temper)* Marion, a bad letter on immigration matters is simply bad. I don't need to tell you that.

Marion: Are they going to be deported?

Eku: *(Ignores the question and heaves another sigh. He is visibly upset)* What life is this we are living?

(Presently, the doorbell rings. Eku gets up, goes to the door and opens it.)

Eku: *(To Ibrahim)* Please come in.

Ibrahim: *(To Marion, in a sombre mood)* My dear sister, it has happened to us at last. We're asked to vacate this country in 14 days!

Marion: *(Shocked)* What!

Ibrahim: Yes! 14 days! There was no warning, not even the slightest hint.

Marion: My Goodness!

Ibrahim: Our tickets and travel documents must have been delivered at the same time. Our neighbours received them on our behalf and delivered the mails to us as soon as we entered the house last night - at about 11.30pm.

Marion: Which of your neighbours?

Ibrahim: The spy…

Eku: My God! *(After a spell of silence)* So, what are we going to do now?

Ibrahim: What can anybody do to avert this?

Eku: *(He ponders for a while)* You mean you're travelling together with Maama and Ansu?

Ibrahim: What else can we do?

Eku: Look here, my friend! If it comes to the crunch, you can appeal through your solicitor. You have the right to appeal against this decision.

Marion: *(Cautiously)* Eku, do you think so?

Eku: My friend, there are a few options available, if you're willing and able.

Marion: What are they?

Eku: To start with, how many more years has Maama got left on the nursing programme?

Ibrahim: This is her final year.

Eku: Bingo! *(Emphatically)* It means that the Home Office cannot deport
Maama. She has the right to complete her studies. And, being her spouse, your visa status could be reviewed with respect to her studentship.

Ibrahim: I am not quite sure about that. Oni's wife is pursuing the same programme. Her husband, himself a former Commonwealth scholarship holder has been deported to Nigeria! Don't ask me why.

Maama: Eku himself knows that non-EU nationals are restricted from taking up full-time employment.

Eku: I know that persons on student visa require a **Work Permit** from the Secretary of State to be able to work in the UK.

Ibrahim: Then, what will I be doing while I wait for Maama to complete her studies? I'm sure that I will not be granted permission to take up employment, paid or unpaid.

Eku: How about leaving Maama and Ansu here in the UK?

Marion: What do you mean? IB should leave his wife and child and travel alone to Nigeria? Who will look after them here? Eku, are you running out of your mind?

Eku: *(Getting frantic)* You couldn't even allow me to finish…

Ibrahim: *(Calming them down)* Marion! Please allow him to finish.

Eku: Before you depart, obtain a return ticket to the UK or, keep the cost of such a ticket safe. By returning home to Nigeria and serving for an academic year or so, you would have fulfilled the requirements of the bond you signed with the University before departing. After completing her studies, Maama will easily get a nursing job as nurses are currently in very high demand. She will then invite you. No immigration officer will refuse you visa.

Marion: What does Maama think about parting from Ibrahim?

Ibrahim: That's the big problem. Maama says that she won't stay in the UK alone. She fears separation and distance may endanger our marriage. I fully support her view. A woman may be easy to replace, but a good woman like my Maama will be difficult to find.

Marion: Those who are lucky to have good wives hardly treasure the wisdom in what you've said…

Eku: *(Ignoring her wife's comment)* and, because you're already married, you can't opt for …

Marion: What, marriage of convenience?

Ibrahim: What kind of marriage do you call marriage of convenience?

Marion: *(sarcastically)* Marrying a British or EU national to avert 'Imigreshon wahala'.

IB: I have no ill-feelings about men who marry women from other cultures. Nonetheless, I believe that intercultural marriages may have serious implications, particularly for the children.

Marion: *(Indignantly)* Tell him that!

Eku: Marion, we are just brainstorming!

Marion: Yes! Brainstorming! What comes out of the mouth when the mind is heated had been conceived when…

Ibrahim: Please! Please! Don't let our own problem affect your own peace of mind.

Marion: I'm sorry, Ibrahim.

Eku: I'm used to this by now, after 20 years!

(Marion eyes Eku annoyingly)

Ibrahim: *(To Eku)* As you yourself noted, another marriage is out of the question. Firstly, it will conflict with my record at the Home Office. I really don't know. …*(He heaves a huge sigh and shakes his head despondently).*

(The lighting becomes dull, then yellowish focusing on Eku who presently sits pensively, lost in his thoughts. There is a long spell of silence)

Eku: Hmmm… What are your views concerning claiming asylum in this country?

Ibrahim: Eku, unlike colleagues whose countries of origin are presently ravaged by civil war or religious conflict, I have no grounds on which to claim asylum in the UK. Besides, I would rather return home and die in poverty, than subject myself to such indignity.

(There is a long spell of silence. Marion is visibly sleepy. Ibrahim too, displays signs of tiredness. He leans over on the sofa. Presently, Eku gazes at the national symbols on the wall, losing himself to fantasy as he does so. Lights fade out on the cast on stage and moments later, brighten on a new setting. It is the bare hall of a Registry. There are only four chairs placed around a table on which is a vase of synthetic flowers of different colours. Also, there is a wedding register, widely open. Eku and Ibrahim, the latter, now a figment of Eku's imagination and known as Abraham, are waiting for Carol (the bride), Carol's own friend or relatives, and the Registrar (all figments of Eku's imagination). Abraham has a bouquet of flowers in his hands while Eku carries a camera on his neck. They are both formally dressed for the occasion. Abraham is nervous and embarrassed while Eku is astonished. The bride is a native English girl. Her nonchalance, like her friend's, Daniel, is exemplified by her outward appearance and manner of speaking).

Eku: IB… forgive me my brother, I can't get used to this new name… By the way, will Carol's parents be attending this occasion at all?

Abraham: I'm not sure. I don't think she wants them to.

Eku: *(Shocked)* But, why not?

Abraham: *(Uneasy)* My brother, you know that this is a personal arrangement between Carol and myself. She may either not want to share the fee with anybody, or she may want to keep the matter under wraps…

Eku: *(After a short pause)* And you call this marriage?

Abraham: *(Mutters indistinct words)*

(Almost simultaneously, Carol and Daniel appear, both of them shabbily dressed. Carol seizes Abraham's right hand pretentiously; she greets Eku.

Daniel walks past them and stands aloof. He gives a wry smile from the side of his mouth).

Carol: *(To Eku)* Hi there.

Eku: Hi

Almost simultaneously, the Registrar emerges from another end of the stage. In contrast, he looks very stern, straight faced and formally dressed).

Registrar: Good morning. *(He walks past them to the only table on stage. He peers into the wedding register, playing with the knob of his pen as he does so. Then suddenly, he calls out)* Mr. Abraham Okuni.

Abraham: Yes, please.

Registrar: And Carol!

Carol: Hi ya

Registrar: Welcome to you all. I presume you're the witnesses *(Referring to Eku and Daniel)*

(Eku and Daniel look at each other, then, nod in approval)

Abraham: Eku is my own witness.

Carol: And Danny is mine.

Registrar: Right! The bride and groom, please! *(Carol and Abraham take their seats at the table)* First, Mr. Okuni. How long have you known each other?

Abrahim: *(Nervous, but summons composure)* One ….

Carol: We've been lovers for a year now.

Registrar: Excuse me! I'm talking to Mr. ….

Abraham: Okuni, please.

Registrar: Mr. Okuni, do you co-habit with Carol?

(Abrahim turns to Carol, searching for an answer.)

Carol: Yes, we do.

Registrar: Okay… Carol, normally, a member of our staff should have visited you to certify that you reside at the same premise. But, I have no reason to doubt your integrity.

(Carol caresses and hugs Abraham, giving him a passionate kiss, as if to strengthen him and reassure the Registrar)

Carol: Are you okay? *(They hold each other's hand firmly)*

Abraham: Yep.

Registrar: Right! Is there any one in this audience who has any reason for which Abraham and Carol should not be united in marriage?

(Eku bows his head, closes his eyes, clenches his fists and gnaws his teeth. There is an eerie silence).

Registrar: It means that we should proceed with this business. Can you move this way? *(Referring to Daniel and Eku, indicating where they should relocate on stage.)* Abraham, do you wish to take Carol as your lawful wedded wife, to love and to cherish, in sickness or in health, for better or for worse, till death do you part?

Ibrahim: I do.

Registrar: Then, please write your name in full, complete this section of the Register and sign here. *(Indicating. Abraham does as requested)*.

Registrar: *(To Carol)* And you Carol. Do you wish to take Abraham as your lawful wedded husband, to love and to cherish, in sickness or in health, for better or for worse, till death do you part?

Carol: I do.

Registrar: Then, please write your full name, complete this section of the Register and sign on the dotted line *(Indicating. Carol does as requested)*.

Registrar: First witness! *(Eku moves to the table, takes one of the available seats. The Registrar indicates the part of the register that Eku should complete. He does so.)* Second witness! *(Daniel moves to the table and takes one of the available seats. The Registrar indicates the part of the register that Daniel should complete. He does so).* Bride and groom, once more! *(Abraham and Carol take their respective places by the Registrar).* By the powers vested in me, I hereby pronounce you husband and wife. Abraham, you may kiss the bride. *(Posing for the camera, Abraham gives the bouquet of flowers, to Carol and accompanies this with a very warm and sensational kiss. Eku takes pictures of the newly wedded in different poses. He also takes pictures of the Registry and others present).*

Lights fade out

The End

GLOSSARY

WORD	MEANING
1. maasa	A flattery word in West African Pidgin for 'boss', 'master' or elder'. In Sierra Leone, 'Di Paa' is more common, whereas in Nigeria, the word 'oga' is used to denote the same meaning.
2. chief	A traditional leader. Today, the term is also used to refer to someone who commands respect among equals.
3. Alhaji	A Muslim who has performed pilgrimage to Mecca
4. chief, doctor, Alhaji	Words of praise heaped on someone who is well known and recognised in a community
5. na waa oo	This is war (This is a difficult battle to be won).
6. Ah jus de oo	I am just surviving
7. oh jare	My dear...
8. whoh'	What
9. garri	Fine grains of cassava produced by using a grater. The grains are then fried in a big open pot or an oven
10. boht how man go do?	What else can one do?
11. Oga, tank you	Elder one, many thanks

plenty plenty.	
12. Yu go sahbi. Yu weit! Yu go know whetha nah kohnflekes or kohl rehs yu go it foh brekfahs when wi go tohn bahk nah wi kohntri.	You will soon find out. You only have to wait and see whether it's cornflakes or leftovers of rice you will be eating for breakfast when we shall return home to our country.
	A type of green commonly used as slimy sauce for foofoo and rice.
13. krenkren	I prefer to eat with my hand as we usually do in my own country.
	dirty
14. I fit eat wit my hand as we go do in my kohntri.	eat
	vegetables
15. doh'ee	This (story about visa restriction) fills my mouth like dry garri (dry garri usually rises when water is added to it).
16. ee'	Deep trouble
17. veggies	
18. Dis wan ful my mouth like dry garri.	
19. wahala	

70

20. nah wetin be dis?	What type of trouble is this?
21. ehdahkeh	Silence! Let's have perfect quietness! A type of musical instrument made of calabash with cowrie shells strung around it.
22. shehgbuleh	
23. oni lu eh behreh	A type of command to musicians or drummers to resume playing.
24. Aunty	Aunt (nowadays, the term is used to refer to all friends and female relatives of one's mother).
25. nah me	It's me.
26. Bwana	Swahili word for 'Mr.'
27. jambo	Swahili word for 'Hello', 'hi', or 'good morning'
28. eke!	My God!
29. Jesus Christ, kohm and hear dis!	Jesus, Christ, come down and listen to this!
30. imigreshon wahala	Problems imposed by immigration restrictions

Printed in the United States
By Bookmasters